Step-by-Step
PROBLEM SOLVING

Grade 3

Frank Schaffer
An imprint of Carson-Dellosa Publishing LLC
Greensboro, North Carolina

Credits

Content Editors: Christine Schwab and Heather Stephan
Copy Editor: Barrie Hoople
Layout and Cover Design: Lori Jackson

This book has been correlated to state, common core state, national, and Canadian provincial standards. Visit *www.carsondellosa.com* to search for and view its correlations to your standards.

Copyright © 2012, SAP Group Pte Ltd

Frank Schaffer
An imprint of Carson-Dellosa Publishing LLC
PO Box 35665
Greensboro, NC 27425 USA
www.carsondellosa.com

ISBN 978-1-60996-478-8
01-335111151

Introduction

The **Step-by-Step Problem Solving** series focuses on the underlying processes and strategies essential to problem solving. Each book introduces various skill sets and builds upon them as the level increases. The six-book series covers the following thinking skills and heuristics:

Thinking Skills
- Analyzing Parts and Wholes
- Comparing
- Classifying
- Identifying Patterns and Relationships
- Deduction
- Induction
- Spatial Visualization

Heuristics
- Act It Out
- Draw a Diagram/Model
- Look for a Pattern
- Work Backward
- Make a List/Table
- Guess and Check
- Before and After
- Make Suppositions
- Use Equations

Students who are keen to develop their problem-solving abilities will learn quickly how to:
- make sense of the problem sum: what am I asked to find?
- make use of given information: what do I know?
- think of possible strategies: have I come across similar problems before?
- choose the correct strategy: apply what I know confidently.
- solve the problem: work out the steps.
- check the answer: is the solution logical and reasonable?

Practice questions follow each skill-set example, and three graded mixed practices (easy, intermediate, challenging) are provided for an overall assessment of the skills learned. The worked solutions show the application of the strategies used. Students will find this series invaluable in helping them understand and master problem-solving skills.

Table of Contents

Strategy Summary

The following summary provides examples of the various skill sets taught in Step-by-Step Problem Solving.

Page 6 Skill Set 1-A: Analyzing Parts and Wholes

Analyzing parts and wholes is a basic and useful way of looking at a problem. To analyze parts and wholes is to recognize the parts and understand how they form the whole.

Example: There are 48 red beads and 59 blue beads in a bag. How many beads are in the bag?

Think
- Identify the parts: 48 red beads and 59 blue beads.
- Identify the whole: total number of beads in the bag.
- Draw the part-whole model.
- Fill in the data to find the answer.

Solve 48   59

48 + 59 = 107

Answer   There are **107 beads** in the bag.

Page 8 Skill Set 1-B: Analyzing Parts and Wholes

Sometimes, a problem gives the whole but not the part. Use the part-whole model to answer the problem.

Example: Pedro has 30 trading cards. He gives 12 of them away. How many trading cards does Pedro have left?

Think
- Identify the whole: 30 total trading cards.
- Identify the parts: 12 given away, ? left.
- Draw the part-whole model.
- Fill in the data to find the answer.

Solve   30

30 − 12 = 18

Answer   Pedro has **18 trading cards** left.

Page 11 Skill Set 2-A: Comparing

Comparing is an effective way of identifying the relationship between the variables

in a problem. Comparing the information in a problem helps us determine the differences in variables' quantities (for example, more or less).

Example: Sam has 12 pencils. Jay has 16 more pencils than Sam. How many pencils does Jay have?

Think
- How many more pencils does Jay have?
- Draw the comparison model.
- Fill in the data to find the answer.

Solve

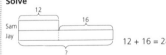

12 + 16 = 28

Answer   Jay has **28 pencils**.

Page 13 Skill Set 2-B: Comparing

Sometimes, a problem involves subtraction instead of addition. Use the comparison model to solve the problem.

Example: There are 33 bolts in a toolbox. There are 15 fewer nuts in the toolbox. How many nuts are in the toolbox?

Think
- How many fewer nuts than bolts are in the toolbox?
- Draw the comparison model.
- Fill in the data to find the answer.

Solve   33

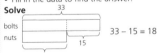

33 − 15 = 18

Answer   There are **18 nuts** in the toolbox.

Page 16 Skill Set 3: Classifying

Classifying means to organize the given data into groups. The data in each group shares common characteristics.

Strategy Summary

The following summary provides examples of the various skill sets taught in Step-by-Step Problem Solving.

Example: Classify the shapes into two groups. Put an equal number of shapes into each group.

Think
• Look for common characteristics: shape (circle or square), pattern (shaded or lines).
• Test the data: shape (5 circles, 3 squares), pattern (4 shaded, 4 with lines).
• Classify the shapes by the type of data that meets the condition "an equal number of shapes in each group."

Answer

Page 19 Skill Set 4: Identifying Patterns and Relationships
In number and pattern sequences, a relationship often exists among the data in the given arrangement. Always check the number or pattern sequence using the four operations (+, −, ×, and ÷), or rotate the patterns to find the relationship among the data.

Example: Draw the shape that comes next.

Think
• Observe the shapes.
• Look for a pattern: rotation, repetition, mirror image.
• Test your guesses and determine the sequence.

Solve

circle   square   circle   square   circle   square

Answer

Page 23 Skill Set 5-A: Act It Out
Act It Out is especially helpful when it is difficult to visualize a given problem. Act out the situation from the problem or use objects to represent the variables in the problem.

Example: The figure below shows 3 squares formed using 10 toothpicks. Rearrange 2 toothpicks so that the figure shows 2 squares.

Think
• Act it out: Use 10 toothpicks to form the given figure.
• Try moving any 2 toothpicks to get the solution.

Solve   **Answer**

2 squares

Page 26 Skill Set 5-B: Act It Out
Besides using concrete items, such as toothpicks and matchsticks, to represent a problem, we can sometimes act out a situation to help solve the problem.

Example: There are 3 men and 3 women in a dance class. For the tango, the men and women need to pair up. How many different pairs can they form?

Think
• Act it out! Get 6 friends, 3 boys and 3 girls, to act out the problem.

Solve
Let the boys be M1, M2, and M3. Let the girls be W1, W2, and W3.

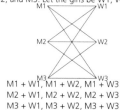

M1 + W1, M1 + W2, M1 + W3
M2 + W1, M2 + W2, M2 + W3
M3 + W1, M3 + W2, M3 + W3

Answer   They can form **9 different pairs**.

Page 28 Skill Set 6-A: Draw a Diagram/Model
Drawing diagrams or models helps us organize the data and identify the relationship among the data in a problem. Similar to Analyzing Parts and Wholes, this skill set involves drawing a different type of model.

Example: A bag of 3 oranges costs $2. How much does Mom pay if she buys 15 oranges?

Think
• Data given: 3 oranges cost $2; Mom buys 15 oranges.
• Can 15 oranges be divided equally into groups of 3?
• Draw a diagram or a model.
• Fill in the data to find the answer.

Solve
Draw a diagram.

15 oranges = 5 groups of 3 oranges

$2 $2 $2 $2 $2

1 group = $2
5 groups = 5 × $2
Draw a model.

3 oranges				
$2	$2	$2	$2	$2

5 × $2 = $10

Answer   Mom pays **$10**.

Page 31 Skill Set 6-B: Draw a Diagram/Model
Some problems require us to relate two sets of data. Draw diagrams or models to help solve these problems.

Example: Mrs. Garcia uses 4 teaspoons of flour and 2 teaspoons of sugar to make a muffin. If she wants to make more muffins and uses 16 teaspoons of flour, how many teaspoons of sugar should she use?

Think
• Data given: 4 teaspoons of flour → 2 teaspoons of sugar
• Can 16 teaspoons of flour be divided equally into groups of 4?
• Draw a model.
• Fill in the data to find the answer.

Solve

4	4	4	4

16 teaspoons of flour

16 ÷ 4 = 4 (groups of teaspoons of flour)
4 groups × 2 teaspoons of sugar = 8 teaspoons of sugar

Answer   She should use **8 teaspoons** of sugar.

Page 32 Skill Set 7: Look for a Pattern
To look for a pattern among the problem's data, examine and test the variables to find the relationship among the data that forms the pattern.

Example: The diagram below shows the net of a cube. What numbers do the stars represent?

Think
• Look at the net of the cube.
• Observe the numbers near 1, 3, and 5.
• Identify the missing numbers.

Answer

The number below 1 is **4**.
The number beside 1 is **3**.

Skill Set 1-A: Analyzing Parts and Wholes

Analyzing parts and wholes is a basic and useful way of looking at a problem. To analyze parts and wholes is to recognize the parts and understand how they form the whole.

Example:
There are 48 red beads and 59 blue beads in a bag. How many beads are in the bag?

 Think
- Identify the parts: 48 red beads and 59 blue beads.
- Identify the whole: total number of beads in the bag.
- Draw the part-whole model.
- Fill in the data to find the answer.

 Solve

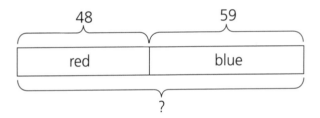

48 + 59 = 107

 Answer There are **107 beads** in the bag.

Give it a try!

There are 21 pens and 17 pencils in a box. How many pens and pencils are in the box?

 Think
Fill in the data to find the answer.

 Solve

_____ + _____ = _____

 Answer There are _____ **pens and pencils** in the box.

(Answer: 38)

Practice: Analyzing Parts and Wholes

1. Catherine has 27 bear stickers and 13 tiger stickers in her album. How many stickers does she have altogether?

💡 **Think**

✏️ **Solve**

⭐ **Answer**

2. Peter reads 39 pages on Monday and 26 pages on Tuesday. How many pages does he read in two days?

💡 **Think**

✏️ **Solve**

⭐ **Answer**

Skill Set 1-B: Analyzing Parts and Wholes

Sometimes, a problem gives the whole but not the part. Use the part-whole model to answer the problem.

Example:
Pedro has 30 trading cards. He gives 12 of them away. How many trading cards does Pedro have left?

 Think
- Identify the whole: 30 total trading cards.
- Identify the parts: 12 given away, ? left.
- Draw the part-whole model.
- Fill in the data to find the answer.

 Solve

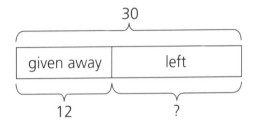

$30 - 12 = 18$

⭐ **Answer** Pedro has **18 trading cards** left.

Give it a try!

In the morning, 45 cars are in a parking lot. By afternoon, 27 have driven off. How many cars are left in the parking lot?

 Think
Fill in the data to find the answer.

 Solve

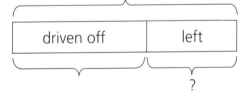

_____ − _____ = _____

⭐ **Answer** There are _____ **cars** left in the parking lot.

(Answer: 18)

3. There are 38 ducks in a pond. Later, 23 of them fly away. How many ducks are left in the pond?

💡 **Think**

✏️ **Solve**

⭐ **Answer**

4. There are 72 children in the hall. Of those children, 48 are boys and the rest are girls. How many girls are in the hall?

💡 **Think**

✏️ **Solve**

⭐ **Answer**

5. There are 85 balls in a basket. The basket contains 27 basketballs and 13 footballs. The rest are volleyballs. How many volleyballs are in the basket?

 Think

Solve

⭐ **Answer**

Skill Set 2-A: Comparing

Comparing is an effective way of identifying the relationship between the variables in a problem. Comparing the information in a problem helps us determine the differences in variables' quantities (for example, more or less).

Example:

Sam has 12 pencils. Jay has 16 more pencils than Sam. How many pencils does Jay have?

 Think
- How many more pencils does Jay have?
- Draw the comparison model.
- Fill in the data to find the answer.

 Solve

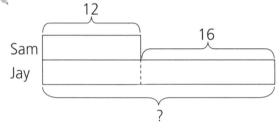

$12 + 16 = 28$

 Answer Jay has **28 pencils**.

Give it a try!

Liza has 18 hair clips. Kayla has 14 more hair clips than Liza. How many hair clips does Kayla have?

 Think
Fill in the data to find the answer.

 Solve

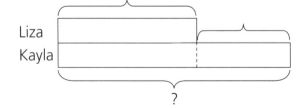

_____ + _____ = _____

 Answer Kayla has _____ **hair clips**.

(Answer: 32)

Practice: Comparing

1. Ginny has 26 local stamps. She has 39 more foreign stamps than local stamps. How many foreign stamps does Ginny have?

💡 **Think**

✏️ **Solve**

⭐ **Answer**

2. There are 35 blue marbles in a bag. There are 24 more red marbles than blue marbles. How many red marbles are in the bag?

💡 **Think**

✏️ **Solve**

⭐ **Answer**

Skill Set 2-B: Comparing

Sometimes, a problem involves subtraction instead of addition. Use the comparison model to solve the problem.

Example:
There are 33 bolts in a toolbox. There are 15 fewer nuts in the toolbox. How many nuts are in the toolbox?

 Think
- How many fewer nuts than bolts are in the toolbox?
- Draw the comparison model.
- Fill in the data to find the answer.

 Solve

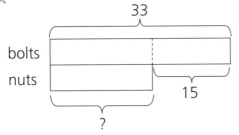

$$33 - 15 = 18$$

⭐ **Answer** There are **18 nuts** in the toolbox.

Give it a try!

There are 41 trees planted along street A. There are 23 fewer trees planted along street B. How many trees are planted along street B?

 Think
Fill in the data to find the answer.

 Solve

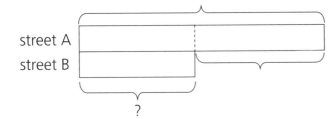

⭐ **Answer** There are _____ **trees** planted along street B.

3. Mr. Lewis bought 56 cans of corn. He bought 27 fewer cans of beans. How many cans of beans did he buy?

💡 **Think**

✏️ **Solve**

⭐ **Answer**

4. Alicia baked 48 muffins. Sasha baked 16 fewer muffins than Alicia. How many muffins did Sasha bake?

💡 **Think**

✏️ **Solve**

⭐ **Answer**

5. Aaron folded 34 paper cranes. Carrie folded 18 fewer paper cranes than Aaron. How many paper cranes did Carrie fold?

 Think

Solve

 Answer

Skill Set 3: Classifying

Classifying means to organize the given data into groups. The data in each group shares common characteristics.

Example:

Classify the shapes into two groups. Put an equal number of shapes into each group.

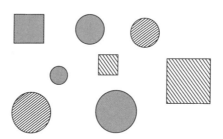

 Think

- Look for common characteristics: shape (circle or square), pattern (shaded or lines).
- Test the data: shape (5 circles, 3 squares), pattern (4 shaded, 4 with lines).
- Classify the shapes by the type of data that meets the condition "an equal number of shapes in each group."

⭐ **Answer**

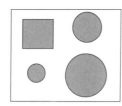

Give it a try!

Classify the figures into three groups. Put an equal number of figures in each group.

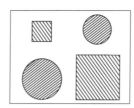

small	medium	large

⭐ **Answer**

 Think

Classify the figures by size.

(Answer: small: ◯ ●, medium: ● ◯, large: ◯ ◯)

Practice: Classifying

1. Classify the figures into two equal groups. Label the groups.

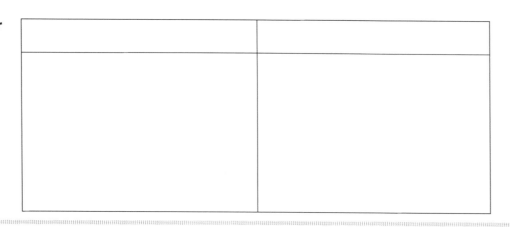

💡 **Think**

⭐ **Answer**

2. Classify the shapes into three groups. Label the groups.

💡 **Think**

⭐ **Answer**

3. Classify the children into two equal groups. Label the groups.

Maddie   Lily   Sabena   Denise   Jenna   Kasey

💡 **Think**

⭐ **Answer**

Skill Set 4: Identifying Patterns and Relationships

In number and pattern sequences, a relationship often exists among the data in the given arrangement. Always check the number or pattern sequence using the four operations (+, −, ×, and ÷), or rotate the patterns to find the relationship among the data.

Example:
Draw the shape that comes next.

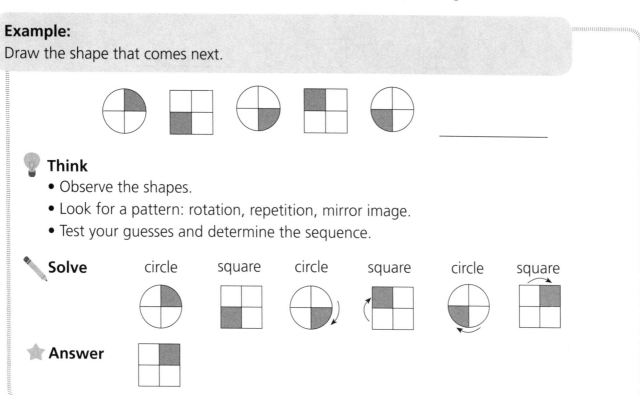

Think
- Observe the shapes.
- Look for a pattern: rotation, repetition, mirror image.
- Test your guesses and determine the sequence.

Solve

circle   square   circle   square   circle   square

Answer

Give it a try!

Draw the 2 shapes that come next.

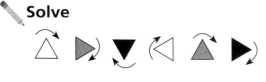

Think

Test your guesses and determine the sequence.

Solve

Answer _____ _____

(Answer: △ ▶)

Practice: Identifying Patterns and Relationships

1. Draw the shape that comes next.

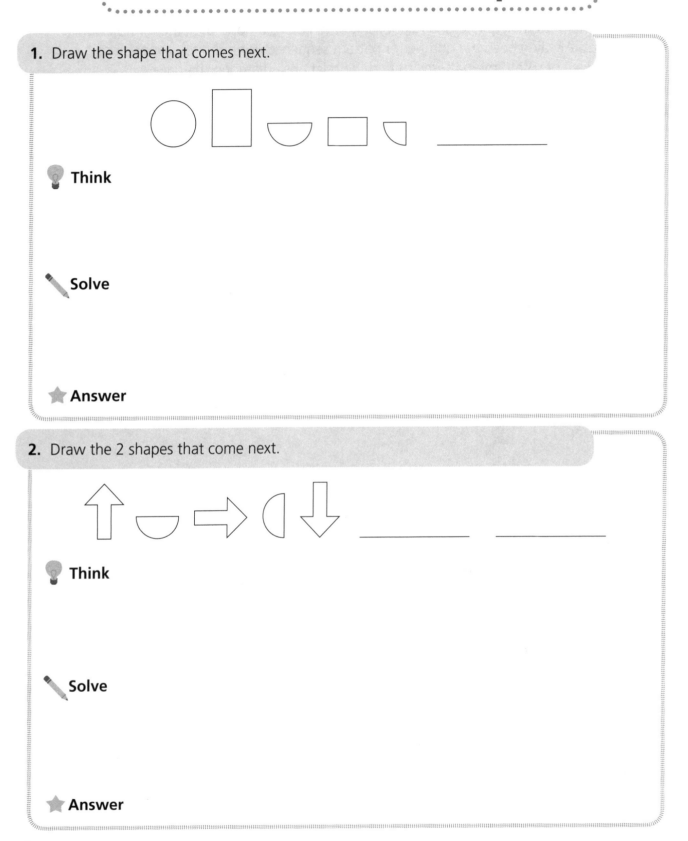

💡 **Think**

🖍 **Solve**

⭐ **Answer**

2. Draw the 2 shapes that come next.

💡 **Think**

🖍 **Solve**

⭐ **Answer**

3. Find the missing number.

 Think

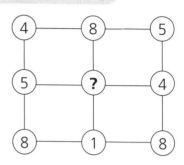

 Solve

 Answer

4. Find the missing number.

 Think

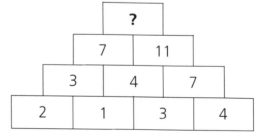

 Solve

 Answer

5. Find the missing numbers.

1	3	4	7	**B**
4	12	16	**A**	36

 Think

 Solve

⭐ **Answer**

Act It Out is especially helpful when it is difficult to visualize a given problem. Act out the situation from the problem or use objects to represent the variables in the problem.

Example:

The figure below shows 3 squares formed using 10 toothpicks. Rearrange 2 toothpicks so that the figure shows 2 squares.

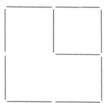

 Think

- Act it out: Use 10 toothpicks to form the given figure.
- Try moving any 2 toothpicks to get the solution.

 Solve

⭐ **Answer**

2 squares

Give it a try!

The figure on the right shows a fish formed using 8 toothpicks. Rearrange 3 toothpicks so that the fish faces the opposite direction.

 Think

Try moving any 3 toothpicks to get the solution.

 Solve

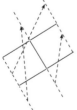

⭐ **Answer**

(Answer:)

Practice: Act It Out

1. The figure below is formed using 12 toothpicks. Remove 2 toothpicks so that the figure shows only 2 squares.

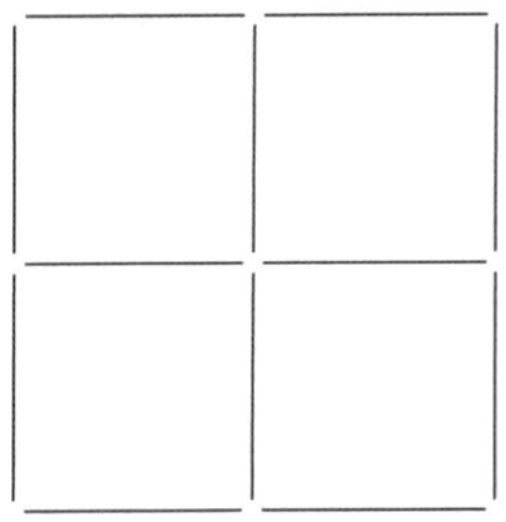

Think

Solve

Answer

2. The figure below is formed using 10 toothpicks. Rearrange 2 toothpicks so that the figure shows 6 squares.

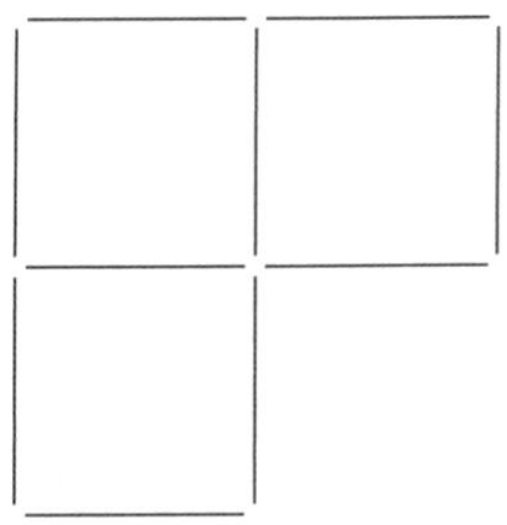

Think

Solve

Answer

3. The figure below is formed using 12 toothpicks. Rearrange 4 toothpicks so that the figure shows 6 triangles.

 Think

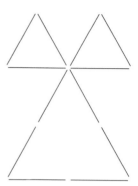

 Solve

 Answer

Besides using concrete items, such as toothpicks and matchsticks, to represent a problem, we can sometimes act out a situation to help solve the problem.

Example:

There are 3 men and 3 women in a dance class. For the tango, the men and women need to pair up. How many different pairs can they form?

 Think

• Act it out! Get 6 friends, 3 boys and 3 girls, to act out the problem.

 Solve

Let the boys be M1, M2, and M3. Let the girls be W1, W2, and W3.

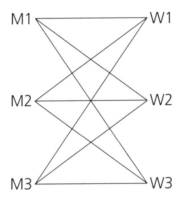

M1 + W1, M1 + W2, M1 + W3

M2 + W1, M2 + W2, M2 + W3

M3 + W1, M3 + W2, M3 + W3

⭐ **Answer** They can form **9 different pairs**.

Challenge yourself!

4. There are 4 girls and 4 boys in a group. The teacher wants 2 students, a girl and a boy, to be group leaders. How many different pairs can the teacher choose?

💡 **Think**

✏️ **Solve**

⭐ **Answer**

5. Uncle Darren prepares 4 different types of sandwich spreads: tuna, egg salad, peanut butter, and chicken salad. He has 3 different types of bread: white, whole grain, and wheat. How many different types of sandwiches can he make if he uses 1 type of spread and 1 type of bread each time?

💡 **Think**

✏️ **Solve**

⭐ **Answer**

Skill Set 6-A: Draw a Diagram/Model

Drawing diagrams or models helps us organize the data and identify the relationship among the data in a problem. Similar to Analyzing Parts and Wholes, this skill set involves drawing a different type of model.

Example:

A bag of 3 oranges costs $2. How much does Mom pay if she buys 15 oranges?

 Think

- Data given: 3 oranges cost $2; Mom buys 15 oranges.
- Can 15 oranges be divided equally into groups of 3?
- Draw a diagram or a model.
- Fill in the data to find the answer.

 Solve

Draw a diagram.

15 oranges = 5 groups of 3 oranges

$2 $2 $2 $2 $2

1 group = $2
5 groups = 5 × $2

Draw a model.

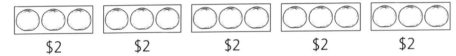

5 × $2 = $10

 Answer Mom pays **$10**.

Give it a try!

A pack of 4 batteries costs $3. How much does Dad pay for 12 batteries?

 Think
Fill in the data to find the answer.

Solve
Draw a model.

___batteries	___batteries	___batteries
$___	$___	$___

?

_____ × _____ = _____

Answer Dad pays _____.

Practice: Draw a Diagram/Model

1. A bag of 5 apples costs $3. How much does Mrs. Lee pay for 10 apples?

💡 **Think**

✏️ **Solve**

⭐ **Answer**

2. A box of 5 snacks costs $2. How much does a teacher pay if she buys 30 snacks for her students?

💡 **Think**

✏️ **Solve**

⭐ **Answer**

3. Hannah has $20. If 12 ounces of walnuts costs $5, how many ounces of walnuts can she buy?

💡 **Think**

✏️ **Solve**

⭐ **Answer**

4. Dad has $50. If 2 pounds of strawberries costs $10, how many pounds of strawberries can he buy?

💡 **Think**

✏️ **Solve**

⭐ **Answer**

Some problems require us to relate two sets of data. Draw diagrams or models to help solve these problems.

Example:

Mrs. Garcia uses 4 teaspoons of flour and 2 teaspoons of sugar to make a muffin. If she wants to make more muffins and uses 16 teaspoons of flour, how many teaspoons of sugar should she use?

 Think

- Data given: 4 teaspoons of flour → 2 teaspoons of sugar
- Can 16 teaspoons of flour be divided equally into groups of 4?
- Draw a model.
- Fill in the data to find the answer.

 Solve

16 teaspoons of flour

16 ÷ 4 = 4 (groups of teaspoons of flour)

4 groups × 2 teaspoons of sugar = 8 teaspoons of sugar

 Answer She should use **8 teaspoons** of sugar.

Challenge yourself!

5. Lily strings groups of 5 red beads and 3 blue beads to make a necklace. If she strings 25 red beads, how many blue beads will she use?

 Think

 Solve

⭐ **Answer**

Skill Set 7: Look for a Pattern

To look for a pattern among the problem's data, examine and test the variables to find the relationship among the data that forms the pattern.

Example:

The diagram below shows the net of a cube. What numbers do the stars represent?

	6	
	5	
2	1	3
	4	

💡 **Think**
- Look at the net of the cube.
- Observe the numbers near 1, 3, and 5.
- Identify the missing numbers.

⭐ **Answer**

	6	
	5	
2	1	3
	4	

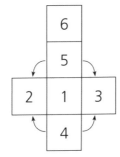

The number below 1 is **4**.

The number beside 1 is **3**.

Give it a try!

The diagram below shows the net of a cube. What numbers do the stars represent?

	1	
2	3	4
	5	
	6	

💡 **Think**
Identify the missing numbers.

⭐ **Answer**

The number below 5 is ____.

The number beside 1 is ____.

(Answers: 6, 4)

1. Study the pattern below. Draw the 2 patterns that come next.

💡 **Think**

✏️ **Solve**

⭐ **Answer** _____   _____

Practice: Look for a Pattern

Use the following information to answer questions 2 and 3.

Emily uses tiles to create the patterns below.

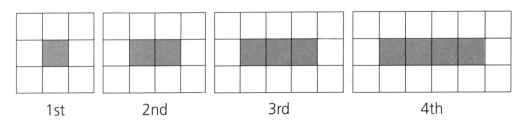

1st   2nd   3rd   4th

2. How many shaded tiles will she use to create the 6th pattern?

💡 **Think**

✏️ **Solve**

⭐ **Answer**

3. How many tiles altogether will she use to create the 6th pattern?

💡 **Think**

✏️ **Solve**

⭐ **Answer**

The diagram below shows the net of a cube. Use the diagram to answer questions 4 and 5.

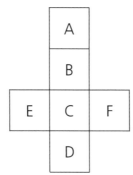

	A	
	B	
E	C	F
	D	

4. What letter does the star represent?

 Think

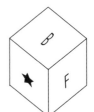

 Solve

⭐ **Answer**

5. What letter does the star represent?

💡 **Think**

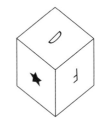

🖍 **Solve**

⭐ **Answer**

1. Aunt Nadia has 36 goldfish and 28 minnows. How many fish does she have altogether?

💡 **Think**

✏️ **Solve**

⭐ **Answer**

2. There are 89 balls in a crate. There are 45 tennis balls and the rest are basketballs. How many basketballs are in the crate?

💡 **Think**

✏️ **Solve**

⭐ **Answer**

3. Sally has 26 books. Her sister has 15 more books than she has. How many books does Sally's sister have?

💡 **Think**

✏️ **Solve**

⭐ **Answer**

4. There are 56 penguins in a zoo. There are 29 fewer otters than penguins. How many otters are there in the zoo?

💡 **Think**

✏️ **Solve**

⭐ **Answer**

5. Classify the objects into two equal groups. Label the groups.

💡 **Think**

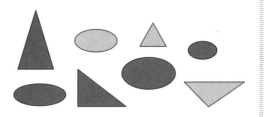

⭐ **Answer**

---

6. Study the pattern. Draw the shape that comes next.

_____

💡 **Think**

⭐ **Answer**

Mixed Practice: Easy

7. The figure below is formed using 8 toothpicks. Rearrange 4 toothpicks so that the figure shows 2 squares.

Think

Solve

Answer

8. Kelly wants to make salads for a party. She has 4 different types of lettuce and 5 different types of dressing. How many different types of salads can she make if she uses 1 type of lettuce and 1 type of dressing each time?

Think

Solve

Answer

9. A store sells 3 potatoes for $1. How much do 15 potatoes cost?

  Think

 **Solve**

⭐ **Answer**

10. Study the pattern. Draw the pattern that comes next.

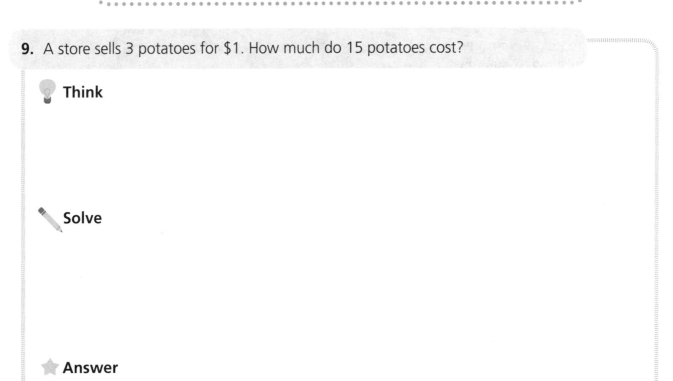

💡 **Think**

✏️ **Solve**

⭐ **Answer**

11. Ashley has 37 pink rubber bands and 47 orange rubber bands. How many rubber bands does she have altogether?

💡 **Think**

✏️ **Solve**

⭐ **Answer**

12. There are 44 birds on a tree. Later, 28 birds fly away. How many birds are left on the tree?

💡 **Think**

✏️ **Solve**

⭐ **Answer**

13. Andre has 38 toys. His brother has 33 more toys than he has. How many toys does Andre's brother have?

💡 **Think**

✏️ **Solve**

⭐ **Answer**

14. There are 40 chicks at a farm. There are 26 fewer ducklings at the farm. How many ducklings are at the farm?

💡 **Think**

✏️ **Solve**

⭐ **Answer**

Mixed Practice: Intermediate

1. A pet store sold 18 fish on Monday and 22 fish on Tuesday. They sold 28 fish on Wednesday. How many fish did the store sell altogether?

💡 **Think**

✏️ **Solve**

⭐ **Answer**

2. Olivia has 99 stickers. She has 34 star stickers and 26 flower stickers. The rest are heart stickers. How many heart stickers does she have?

💡 **Think**

✏️ **Solve**

⭐ **Answer**

Mixed Practice: Intermediate

3. Store A sold 28 cards. Store A sold 32 fewer cards than Store B.
A. How many cards did Store B sell?
B. How many cards did both stores sell altogether?

Think

Solve

Answer

4. There are two numbers. The first number is 6 more than the second number. The sum of the two numbers is 30. What are the numbers?

Think

Solve

Answer

5. Study the pattern below. Draw the shape that comes next.

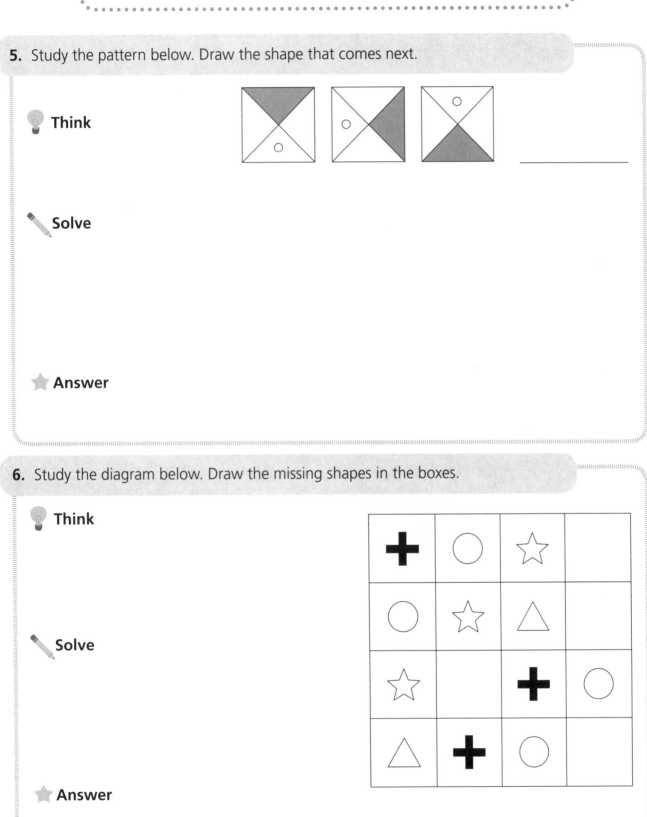

💡 **Think**

✏️ **Solve**

⭐ **Answer**

6. Study the diagram below. Draw the missing shapes in the boxes.

💡 **Think**

✏️ **Solve**

⭐ **Answer**

7. Find the next two numbers in the pattern.

💡 **Think**

1	2	3	5	8		

✏️ **Solve**

⭐ **Answer**

8. A store sells white paint in cans of 1 gallon, 2 gallons, 5 gallons, and 10 gallons. Mr. Shaw needs 20 gallons of white paint. He does not want to buy more than 5 cans of paint. How many different combinations of cans of paint can he choose?

💡 **Think**

✏️ **Solve**

⭐ **Answer**

9. A store sells 3 mints for 20 cents. Maria paid 80 cents for some mints. If she shared them equally with her sister, how many mints did each sister get?

💡 **Think**

✏️ **Solve**

⭐ **Answer**

10. Ty is the 5th person in a line. Libby is 4th from the end of the line. If 4 children are standing between Ty and Libby, how many children are in the line altogether?

💡 **Think**

✏️ **Solve**

⭐ **Answer**

Mixed Practice: Intermediate

11. Juan has 95 marbles. He has 21 white marbles and 32 black marbles. The rest of the marbles are blue. How many blue marbles does he have?

Think

Solve

Answer

12. Grocer A sold 34 eggs. Grocer B sold 17 more eggs than Grocer A.
A. How many eggs did Grocer B sell?
B. How many eggs did both grocers sell altogether?

Think

Solve

Answer

13. Classify the objects into three equal groups. Label the groups.

💡 **Think**

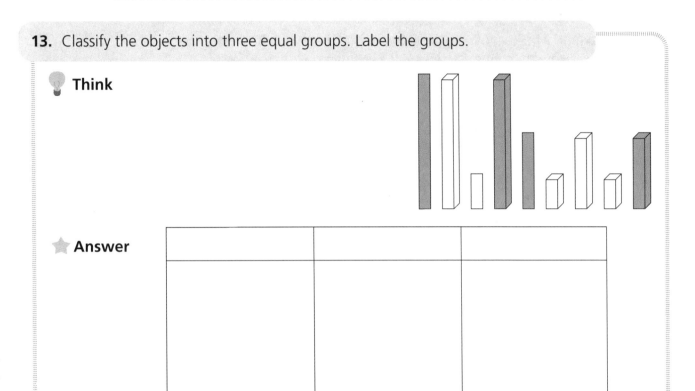

⭐ **Answer**

14. Find the next three numbers in the pattern.

1	2	3	6	11			

💡 **Think**

✏️ **Solve**

⭐ **Answer**

1. Mrs. Beck and Mrs. Irving have $100 in all. Mrs. Beck has $20 more than Mrs. Irving. How much money does each woman have?

 Think

 Solve

⭐ **Answer**

2. A total of 24 ducks, chickens, and geese live on a farm. There are 6 more chickens than ducks and 6 more geese than ducks. How many ducks live on the farm?

 Think

 Solve

 Answer

3. Study the patterns carefully. Find the missing number.

 Think

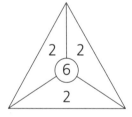 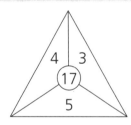 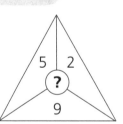

 Solve

 Answer

Mixed Practice: Challenging

4. Taylor has 2 T-shirts: 1 yellow and 1 red. He has 2 pairs of pants: 1 blue and 1 black. He has 2 caps: 1 green and 1 purple. How many different outfits can he make altogether?

Think

Solve

Answer

5. A group of 2 angelfish and 3 goldfish costs $8. Jane wants to buy several groups for a total of 20 fish altogether. How much does she need to pay?

Think

Solve

Answer

6. How many more triangles must be shaded so that $\frac{3}{4}$ of the figure is shaded?

 Think

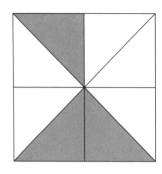

✏️ **Solve**

⭐ **Answer**

7.

$$\triangle \times \square = 24$$

$$\triangle + \square = 10$$

$$\triangle + \square + \bigstar = 19$$

What is $\bigstar + \square$?

💡 **Think**

✏️ **Solve**

⭐ **Answer**

8. Holly has 4 apples. Zack has 3 times as many apples as Holly. Greg has 5 fewer apples than Zack.

A. How many apples does Greg have?

B. How many apples do the 3 children have altogether?

 Think

Solve

Answer

9. Mom mixes 200 milliliters of frozen orange juice with 300 milliliters of water to make orange juice. How much water does she need if she uses 600 milliliters of frozen orange juice?

 Think

Solve

 Answer

10. Study the pattern below. Draw the 2 patterns that come next.

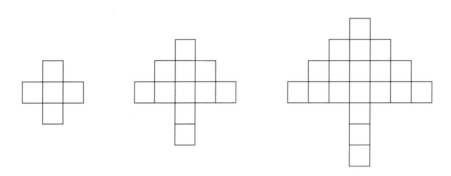

 Think

 Solve

⭐ **Answer**

11. Study the patterns carefully. Find the missing number.

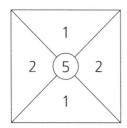 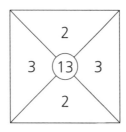 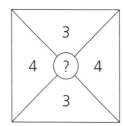

💡 **Think**

✏️ **Solve**

⭐ **Answer**

12. A sports team is made up of 6 boys and 4 girls. How many boys must a school send for a sports competition if it wants to send 28 girls?

💡 **Think**

✏️ **Solve**

⭐ **Answer**

Analyzing Parts and Wholes

Pages 6–10

1.

27	13
bear	tiger

27 + 13 = 40
She has **40 stickers** altogether.

2.

39	26
Monday	Tuesday

39 + 26 = 65
He reads **65 pages** in two days.

3.

38

fly away	left
23	?

38 − 23 = 15
There are **15 ducks** left in the pond.

4.

72

boys	girls
48	?

72 − 48 = 24
There are **24 girls** in the hall.

5.

85

basketballs	footballs	volleyballs
27	13	?

basketballs + footballs → 27 + 13 = 40
volleyballs → 85 − 40 = 45
There are **45 volleyballs** in the basket.

Comparing

Pages 11–15

1.

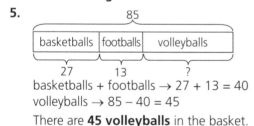

26 + 39 = 65
Ginny has **65 foreign stamps**.

2.

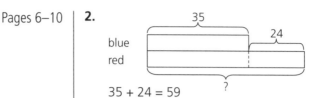

35 + 24 = 59
There are **59 red marbles** in the bag.

3.

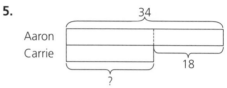

56 − 27 = 29
He bought **29 cans** of beans.

4.

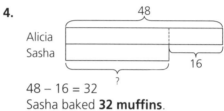

48 − 16 = 32
Sasha baked **32 muffins**.

5.

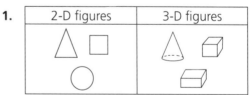

34 − 18 = 16
Carrie folded **16 paper cranes**.

Classifying

Pages 16–18

1.

2-D figures	3-D figures
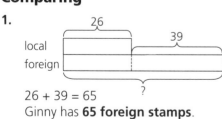	

2.

light shading	medium shading	dark shading

3.

white shoes	black shoes
Maddie	Lily
Denise	Sabena
Kasey	Jenna

Identifying Patterns and Relationships

Pages 19–22

1.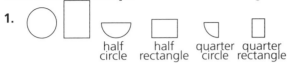

   half circle   half rectangle   quarter circle   quarter rectangle

2.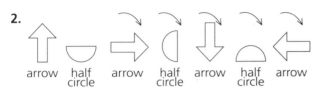

   arrow   half circle   arrow   half circle   arrow   half circle   arrow

3.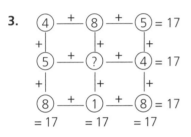

   $17 - 5 - 4 = 8$

   $17 - 8 - 1 = 8$

   The missing number is **8**.

4.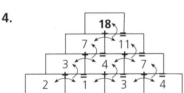

   The missing number is **18**.

5.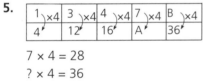

   $7 \times 4 = 28$

   $? \times 4 = 36$

   $? = 9$

   A = 28, B = 9

Act It Out

Pages 23–27

1.

   (Accept other correct answers.)

2.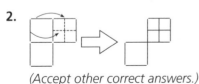

   (Accept other correct answers.)

3.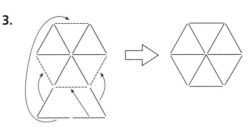

4. Let the boys be b1, b2, b3, and b4.
   Let the girls be g1, g2, g3, and g4.

   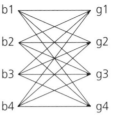

   b1 + g1, b1 + g2, b1 + g3, b1 + g4,
   b2 + g1, b2 + g2, b2 + g3, b2 + g4,
   b3 + g1, b3 + g2, b3 + g3, b3 + g4,
   b4 + g1, b4 + g2, b4 + g3, b4 + g4.
   or
   $4 \times 4 = 16$
   The teacher can choose **16 different pairs**.

5.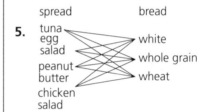

   spread   bread

   tuna + white, tuna + whole grain, tuna + wheat,
   egg salad + white, egg salad + whole grain,
   egg salad + wheat,
   peanut butter + white, peanut butter + whole grain,
   peanut butter + wheat,
   chicken salad + white, chicken salad + whole grain,
   chicken salad + wheat
   or
   $4 \times 3 = 12$
   He can make **12 different types of sandwiches**.

Draw a Diagram/Model

Pages 28–31

1.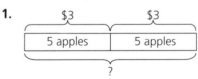

   10 apples = 2 bags of 5 apples
   $\$3 \times 2 = \$6$
   She pays **$6**.

2.

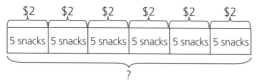

30 snacks $= 6$ groups of 5 snacks
$\$2 \times 6 = \$12$
She pays **$12**.

3.

$\$20 \div \$5 = 4$ (groups of 12 ounces)
4×12 ounces $= 48$ ounces
She can buy **48 ounces** of walnuts.

4.

$\$50 \div \$10 = 5$ (groups of 2 pounds)
5×2 pounds $= 10$ pounds
He can buy **10 pounds** of strawberries.

5.

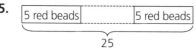

$25 \div 5 = 5$ (groups of red beads)
5 groups $\times 3$ blue beads $= 15$ blue beads
She will use **15 blue beads**.

Look for a Pattern

Pages 32–35

1. The given pattern:

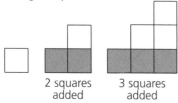

2 squares added   3 squares added

The next 2 patterns in the sequence:

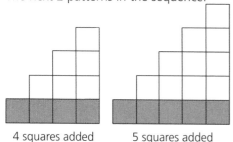

4 squares added   5 squares added

2. 1st pattern → 1 shaded tile
2nd pattern → 2 shaded tiles
3rd pattern → 3 shaded tiles
4th pattern → 4 shaded tiles
5th pattern → 5 shaded tiles
6th pattern → 6 shaded tiles
She will use **6 shaded tiles**.

3. 1st pattern → 8 white tiles
2nd pattern → 10 white tiles $+2$
3rd pattern → 12 white tiles $+2$
4th pattern → 14 white tiles $+2$
5th pattern → 16 white tiles $+2$
6th pattern → 18 white tiles $+2$
18 white $+ 6$ shaded $= 24$ tiles
She will use **24 tiles** altogether.

4. **C**

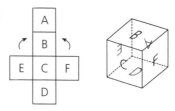

5. **A**

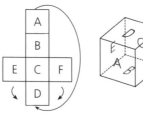

Mixed Practice: Easy

Pages 36–42

1.

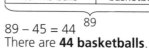

$36 + 28 = 64$
She has **64 fish** altogether.

2.

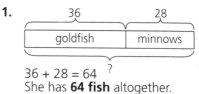

$89 - 45 = 44$
There are **44 basketballs**.

3.

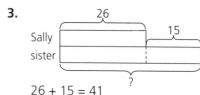

$26 + 15 = 41$
Sally's sister has **41 books**.

4.

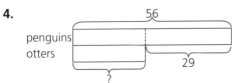

56 − 29 = 27
There are **27 otters** in the zoo.

5.

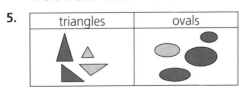

triangles	ovals

6.

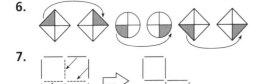

7.

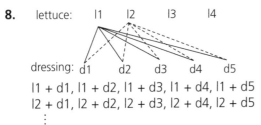

(Accept other correct answers.)

8. lettuce: l1   l2   l3   l4

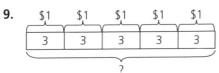

dressing: d1   d2   d3   d4   d5

l1 + d1, l1 + d2, l1 + d3, l1 + d4, l1 + d5
l2 + d1, l2 + d2, l2 + d3, l2 + d4, l2 + d5
⋮

4 types of lettuce × 5 types of dressing = 20
She can make **20 different types of salads**.

9.

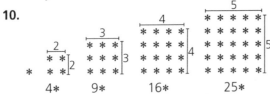

15 potatoes = 5 groups of 3 potatoes
5 × \$1 = \$5
They cost **\$5**.

10.

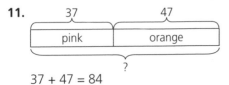

4∗   9∗   16∗   25∗

11.

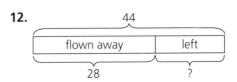

37 + 47 = 84
She has **84 rubber bands** altogether.

12.

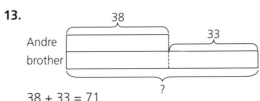

44 − 28 = 16
There are **16 birds** left on the tree.

13.

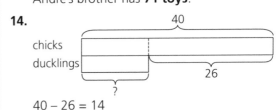

38 + 33 = 71
Andre's brother has **71 toys**.

14.

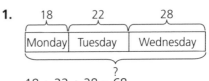

40 − 26 = 14
There are **14 ducklings** at the farm.

Mixed Practice: Intermediate   Pages 43–49

1.

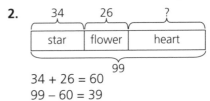

18 + 22 + 28 = 68
The store sold **68 fish** altogether.

2.

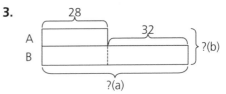

34 + 26 = 60
99 − 60 = 39
She has **39 heart stickers**.

3.

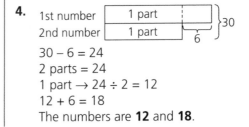

A. 28 + 32 = 60
Store B sold **60 cards**.

B. 60 + 28 = 88
Both stores sold **88 cards** altogether.

4. 1st number | 1 part |
2nd number | 1 part | }30 6

30 − 6 = 24
2 parts = 24
1 part → 24 ÷ 2 = 12
12 + 6 = 18
The numbers are **12** and **18**.

5.

6. Each row has 4 different shapes

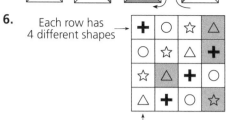

✚	○	☆	△
○	☆	△	✚
☆	△	✚	○
△	✚	○	☆

Each column has 4 different shapes.

7.

| 1 | 2 | 3 | 5 | 8 | **13** | **21** |

1+1 1+2 2+3 3+5 5+8 8+13

The numbers are **13** and **21**.

8. 10 liters + 10 liters = 20 liters
10 liters + 5 liters + 5 liters = 20 liters
10 liters + 5 liters + 2 liters + 2 liters + 1 liters = 20 liters
5 liters + 5 liters + 5 liters + 5 liters = 20 liters
He can choose **4 different combinations**.

9. 20 cents

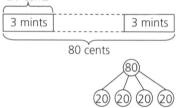

80 cents = 4 groups of 20 cents
4 × 3 mints = 12 mints
12 ÷ 2 = 6
Each sister got **6 mints**.

10.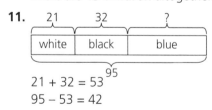

There are **13 children** altogether.

11.

| 21 | 32 | ? |
| white | black | blue |

95
21 + 32 = 53
95 − 53 = 42
He has **42 blue marbles**.

12.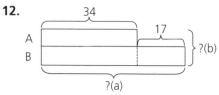

A. 34 + 17 = 51
Grocer B sold **51 eggs**.
B. 51 + 34 = 85
Both grocers sold **85 eggs** altogether.

13.

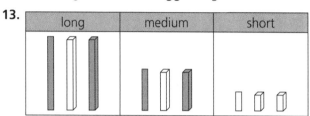

| long | medium | short |

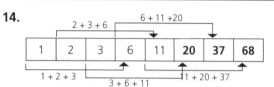

14.

2 + 3 + 6   6 + 11 + 20

| 1 | 2 | 3 | 6 | 11 | **20** | **37** | **68** |

1 + 2 + 3   3 + 6 + 11   1 + 20 + 37

The numbers are **20**, **37**, and **68**.

Mixed Practice: Challenging   Pages 50–56

1.

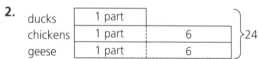

Mrs. Beck | 1 part |
Mrs. Irving | 1 part | $20 } $100

2 parts → $100 − $20 = $80
1 part → $80 ÷ 2 = $40 (Mrs. Irving)
$40 + $20 = $60 (Mrs. Beck)
Mrs. Irving has **$40** and Mrs. Beck has **$60**.

2.

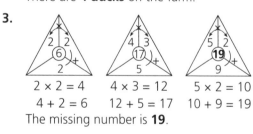

ducks | 1 part |
chickens | 1 part | 6
geese | 1 part | 6 } 24

24 − 6 − 6 = 12
3 parts = 12
1 part → 12 ÷ 3 = 4
There are **4 ducks** on the farm.

3.

2 × 2 = 4   4 × 3 = 12   5 × 2 = 10
4 + 2 = 6   12 + 5 = 17   10 + 9 = 19
The missing number is **19**.

4.

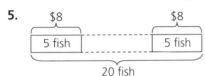

T-shirts	pants	caps
yellow	blue	green
red	black	purple

If he wears his yellow T-shirt, he can make 4 outfits.

If he wears his red T-shirt, he can make 4 outfits.

He can make **8 outfits altogether**.

5.

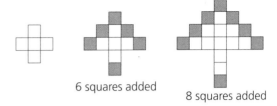

20 ÷ 5 = 4 (groups of fish)

4 × $8 = $32

She needs to pay **$32**.

6. There are 8 triangles in the figure.

$$\frac{3}{4} = \frac{6}{8}$$

6 triangles need to be shaded.

6 − 3 = 3

Shade any **3 triangles**.

7. △ × □ = 24 → { 2 × 12 = 24 (✗)
3 × 8 = 24 (✗)
6 × 4 = 24 (✓)

△ + □ = 10 → { 6 + 4 = 10

△ + □ + ✱ = 19
(the △ + □ braced as 10)

✱ = 19 − 10 = 9

✱ + □ = 9 + 4 = 13 (if △ = 6, □ = 4)

or

✱ + □ = 9 + 6 = 15 (if △ = 4, □ = 6)

✱ + □ = **13** or **15**.

8.

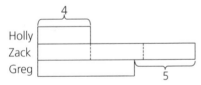

A. Zack → 4 × 3 = 12

Greg → 12 − 5 = 7

Greg has **7 apples**.

B. 4 + 12 + 7 = 23

The three children have **23 apples** altogether.

9.

200 mL	200 mL	200 mL

600 mL of frozen orange juice

600 mL ÷ 200 mL = 3 (groups of frozen orange juice)

3 groups × 300 mL of water = 900 mL of water

She uses **900 milliliters** of water.

10.

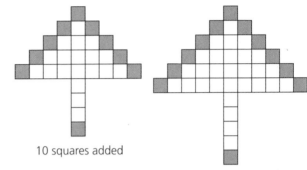

6 squares added   8 squares added

The next 2 patterns in the sequence:

10 squares added

12 squares added

11.

1 + 2 = 3   2 + 3 = 5   3 + 4 = 7

3 × 1 = 3   5 × 2 = 10   7 × 3 = 21

3 + 2 = 5   10 + 3 = 13   21 + 4 = 25

The missing number is **25**.

12.

4	4	4	4	4	4	4

28 girls

28 ÷ 4 = 7 (groups of girls)

7 groups × 6 boys = 42 boys

The school must send **42 boys**.